Keeper of the Night

by Milo Mason

illustrated by Anna Vojtech

MODERN CURRICULUM PRESS

Pearson Learning Group

In a galaxy far away, there once was a world very much like ours. People like us lived there. This world had a moon like ours too. And on that moon lived Mim.

Mim's full name was the Man in the Moon. Since that was such a long name to say, Mim decided to use his initials instead. But *Tmitm* was a bit hard to pronounce. So the Man in the Moon dropped a few initials.

That left *Mim*. And Mim he was.

Mim was the Keeper of the Night.

Mim was never alone on the moon. With him lived a horse named Argenta. Mim could not have done his work without her.

Argenta was an amazing horse. She was like other horses, only she had two heads, two necks, and two manes. The manes were silver, like her coat, but much brighter. Her bridles were even more beautiful than her manes. Mim had made the bridles himself from star dust mixed with gold.

Most horses are fast. But Argenta could run faster than any other horse.
She could also fly.

In that part of the universe, a great wind roared through space every night, blowing dust off all the stars. Most of this dust eventually landed on the moon.

All star dust is made of light, of course. Where the dust settled, the moon became bright. By the end of a month, the cold moon was covered with glittering star dust. This was the time of the full moon.

Mim loved the moon, and he took good care
of it.

When the moon was full, he began
sweeping. He had a special broom made with
hairs from Argenta's manes.

As Mim swept up the star dust, bit by bit,
the moon became dark once more.

Mim worked hard. He'd sweep, sweep, sweep for days in a steady rhythm. He was very careful. He made sure he swept every speck of the star dust into a gigantic black sack.

It took Mim a month to sweep up all the star dust. Once he finished, the moon was dark again. That was the time of the new moon.

This was everyone's favorite moon, because when the moon was dark, they could see more stars.

When Mim's sack was full of star dust, he loaded it onto Argenta's back. (Light is very light, so the sack was not heavy.) Then Mim climbed up on his horse and gathered the reins of her golden bridles. Together they flew into space.

Sometimes the great black sack got a tiny hole. Some star dust would fall out, making shooting stars.

Mim and Argenta flew to stars that had
grown dim because they had lost too much star
dust. Mim would make the stars bright again
by pouring star dust onto them.

Argenta was a fast horse. But even so, it took
as long as a week to reach the farthest stars.

Mim made sure that he was back on the moon before a month had passed. He had to be. By then, the moon was always covered with star dust again.

As soon as Mim returned, he got right back to work. Out came the broom made with hairs from Argenta's manes.

Again Mim swept until he had swept the moon clean of star dust.

And so it went, month after month. Mim's work never ended.

Why did Mim do it? Why did he sweep if he was just going to have to sweep all over again?

Mim swept the moon to keep it from
gathering dust before it got as bright as the sun.
He was the Keeper of the Night, and his job
was very important. You see, night balances the
day. Mim knows this very well. People, plants,
and animals need night so they can rest. All of
life needs night.

But there was a simpler reason why Mim
worked so hard.

For as much as he loved the moon, he loved
the starlight even more.